How to Play Golf For Beginners

A Guide to Learn the Golf Rules, Etiquette, Clubs, Balls, Types of Play, & A Practice Schedule

Table of Contents

Introduction

Welcome newbie and thank you very much for your interesting in reading this golf book. We have named it "From zero to Hero" as it is intended for people who have never played golf in their lives and now, want to become a part of it.

First, let us start by telling you that you have made a great choice, golf is a beautiful and healthy sport that you can almost play it for the rest of your life. We are not going to lie to you; there will be times in which you will not agree with this sport, this may happen more times than the times you agree with it. But there is a reason why golf is so popular and has been for so many centuries (that's right, centuries) and all around the world.

In this book, we will go over all of the spectrum that you should know before your first stroke, we will go through rules, etiquette, equipment, how the game is played, scoring, different types of playing, beginners tips and finally a conclusion which will be similar to this one right here: Go, start, golf is a journey, not a destination, begin it as soon as possible and never let it end.

Even though we will go through some basic tips and other helpful data, the only thing we will not go into will be the golf technique, as this requires a whole other book with much more pictures, videos, etc. But we will let you know how you can learn the techniques and what to look for in a good golf teacher.

Since we have so many topics to go over we may back and forth on some subjects, as sometimes they are actually important for more than one subject, however please feel free to browse our index in case you either want to go to a specific part of the book or even better just re-reading a part you loved.

Ok, here we go, as they will tell you on the first hole:

GO AHEAD, AND GOOD LUCK!

Quick overview

Golf is one of the oldest sports in the world. Like every sport, its origin is always questionable and may have more than one cable to follow. However, let's start from the point of consensus.

Golf started in Scotland in the 15th century. It is played on a course that has 18 of what the game called holes (most of the times, there can be golf courses with nine holes, 14, etc.), and the main objective is to sink the golf ball into the hole in the fewer number of strokes possible. The courses have different sort of obstacles and lengths to complicate the design.

We are going to explain detailly most of the things we mention in this overview, but for now, it is good enough to understand that every time the golfer hits the ball it counts as a stroke, there is no way around this. The attempt to hit the ball, meaning the action of moving the club to hit the ball is called a swing. The ball can be hit only once per stroke, and the golfer can choose from a different variety of clubs that will result in different shots. The main difference is the distance in which the will go after each stroke.

After each stroke, the golfer will walk towards the ending of the ball and hit it again and again until it is finally sunk on the hole. He is never allowed to move the ball or picked it up; the hole must be finished with the same ball that started (Exceptions are possible, but we will go there in a few chapters).

As a general rule, there are two main ways of playing golf. One is what golfers call "Stroke Play" (Sometimes Medal Play), the other is called "Match Play," it is interesting to remark that golf was played initially in "Match Play" version, it was after some years that Stroke play began.

Stroke play is when the golfer counts his strokes individually from the first hole all the way up to the last, so after a golf round, he may have hit the ball 80, 90, 100 or more times. In this particular way, on a regular day of golf, all of the golfers can play versus each other at different times as they are playing to see who finishes the golf course in fewer strokes, afterword's the just write the result on a board and whoever has the lowest wins.

Match Play is a completely different version (Style wise), two golfers play versus each other at the same time (They can see the other golfer play and know how many strokes they have already hit the ball). They play on a "win the hole bases." This means that after each hole, the player who shot the lowest number of strokes wins the hole and one point. They play the whole 18 holes and whoever wins the most, wins. In this way, it can happen that the match finishes before the 18 holes, for example, a golfer can be 5 points ahead of its contestant and only 4 holes to go, this means that even if said golfer loses all 4 holes remaining, he will still be 1 hole ahead, in this case, the match is abandoned at that time with a winner. In this case, it would be at the end of hole 14 (They do not play holes 15, 16, 17, 18).

There are several other ways to play golf, but this is enough for the overview. Let's now go into rules and etiquette.

Golf Rules and Etiquettes

From the abstract part of golf, this is probably the most important that you will find in the game.

Both golf rules and etiquette are equally important.

Rules are very important not only because they will allow you to play the game properly, but because they will prevent you from getting stroke penalties for doing the wrong thing. This may sound as not so bad, but once you become a golfer you will see that each stroke hurts like a stroke!

Etiquette rules or guidelines are equally important. Golf is a very traditional sport, played by gentlemen and most of the courses are either private golf courses or very high-end public courses. Either way, you must know the etiquette rules and guidelines to enter the world of golf as a gentleman and not just a guy who bought some golf clubs and start hitting the little ball.

Rules

Golf is a very complex sport with lots of rules. Since this is just a basic guide, we are not going to go throughout all the rules as it will just confuse you more than it will help you. Every golfer should buy and read the entire Golf's Rules Book as it is showing respect for the sport.

Also, have in mind that most clubs require knowing the rules before admitting a new member and the associations that give the "Handicap" to the golfers.

However, we want to give you a quick overview of what you can and can't-do.

The most important rule is by far that you are not allowed to touch (move, kick, etc.) the golf ball once it has been played in a hole until it has been sinking into the hole. Why is this rule so important? Because it aims to the spirit of the sport. Almost all the time, nobody will be looking at what you do, this means that cheating in golf is very easy. However, this is a gentlemen sport, that is why it almost never happens, and if it happens and the golfer gets caught, he will face a ban on the sports that can last more than 100 years.

Other important rules are:

- Golfers cannot agree to dismissed or disobey rules.
- The ball must be hit once per swing. It cannot be hit two times, neither "Spooning the ball" is allowed (It would be any action in which the ball is put into the club and then push from there).
- If the golfer breaks any rule and this involves in a penalty, he must tell the rest of the group even if nobody saw what happen
- If you swing the ball with the intention of hitting it and you missed the ball, it counts as a stroke even if the ball hasn't moved an inch.

Then all the remaining rules are mainly about how the sport is played like we said, golfers should go to the official Rules Book and read it completely.

Etiquette

We like to call them "Etiquette Guidelines" instead of rules, as most of them are not a rule that you will find in the official Golf Rules Book.

First and most important, etiquette dictates that a golfer should never do something to disturb another golfer when he is playing. This includes moving around, talking, using the cellphone, practice swings close to him, etc. This is very important, as golfers need a lot of concentration when hitting the ball, plus most of them have a routine that can take almost up to a minute to hit the ball just once.

The next etiquette guideline aims to have and comply with the golf dress code. In general golf clubs have very strict dress codes, and if a golfer or a friend of a golfer is not wearing appropriate golf clothes, he may not be allowed to play the course, even if it is his first time. Every club may have different rules but here are some general rules that apply to most of the clubs in the world:

Men:

- No jeans
- No shorts
- T-shirts must have necks and cannot be sleeveless

- Golf shoes without hard spikes
- No big brands, or sports club's shirts (Like football)

Women:

- Shirt's must have either sleeves or neck
- No jeans
- No shorts

The Handicap

You probably heard or realized that golfers from all ages and level could compete in the same tournament, this means that there is some advantage that is given by the best golfers towards the worst, but, have you ever wonder how it works? How is it called?

This is probably one of the hardest concepts to learn if you have never played golf, but of course, we are going to try.

After they have been playing for a while (The more, the better), it happens that the golfer's score starts to get a tendency towards the same result. For example, in the beginning, it is quite common for golfers to either shot 100 or 125 strokes on a regular day. If you consider hard math, this is not only 25 strokes difference but also a 25% difference. However, the better the golfer gets, it starts happening that this range starts to become smaller and smaller until there is a time (About when they regularly break 100) that they almost always shot around the same number. For example, a golfer who tends to shoot 90, may shoot 87 or 93 but it is extremely weird for him to shoot 80 or 105. Furthermore, if they shot around 80, they shoot in between 75 and 85. This means that after a while you can estimate how many shots each golfer takes.

Thus, to make the sport more fair and competitive, golf has what it is called "The handicap." The history of the word comes from the ancient times in which the knights would fight on horses with very long swords running straight towards each other. If one were better than the other one, he would put a

"Hand in Cap" to have a fairer battle. The Handicap is the same; it is an advantage that is given.

Like we said before, when golfers start to become better they start having similar results (for the reason that it makes no sense to explain right now) let's say that to that number they have to subtract 72, and the result will be his handicap. It means that if a golfer tends to shoot 100, his handicap would be 28 (100-72= 28), then if another tends to shoot 75, his handicap would be 3 (75-72=3). The result without handicap it is called a "gross score," and with a handicap, it is called "Net score." This means that if they want, they can forget about the gross score and just play together just considering the net score, (Even though the Handicap 3 golfer is much better than the 28) and still can have a decent and fun match. It can happen that a golfer shoots 78 gross, 73 net (Handicap 5) and another shoots 89 gross, 70 net (Handicap 19) and in that tournament, the second golfer won even though he hit the golf ball 11 more times than his competitor.

We are not going to get into specific details of how it is calculated but here are just a few notes on how it works:

- Only official associations can take golfers handicap (Every golfer has like a handicap ID number that is unique to him)
- It depends on the association, but most of them consider the best eight rounds of the last 16.
- For the golf round to be considered for handicap, it must be an official club tournament; friendly rounds do not count (Even if you follow all the golf rules)

- Since golf courses have different levels of difficulty, there is what it is called a differential or slope that adjust the final number to a fairer number.

Golf Gear and Equipment

In this chapter, we are going to explain you the most important things that you should know about golf gear and equipment.

Golf Clubs

The Golf Associations are very specific on which clubs you are allowed to play, every year they release a huge list with all of the models that are accepted. This list is not very useful, to make it simple, any club you buy from an official store or pro-shop will be ok.

Like we have been saying, golfers hit the golf ball with a swing that it is made with a golf club. There are many different kinds of golf brands and golf clubs, however, since this is a beginner's book, the idea is that we go over the basics. Also, we are going to explain everything from a generic point of view, without going into specific brands.

What you should know about a golf club is that it has three main parts:

- The grip, where the golfer holds the club.

- The shaft that unites the grip with the face of the club.
- The club face, the part that will hit the ball.

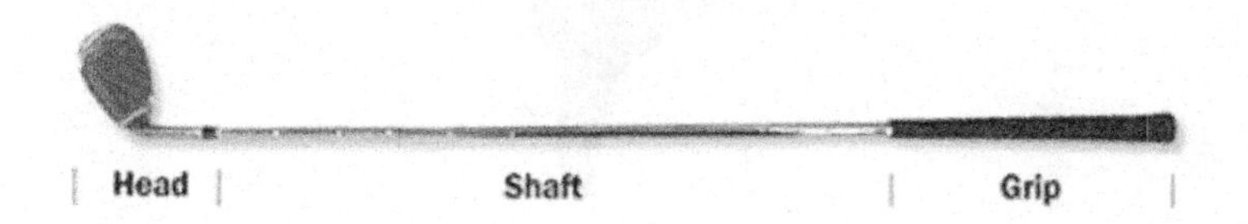

The two main difference that clubs have with each other is the length of the shaft and the openness of the club face; this last one is referring to as "Loft." To know which club in which they have numbers, the smaller the number, the longer the ball should go. Then for some specific shots, they will have letters, in these cases, there is no general rule as to which club hits the ball farther. And finally there is a club call putter which has no loft, and it is used to roll the ball into the hole.

Also, the golf rules specify that a golfer can only have a maximum of fourteen clubs in its bag (with no minimum), so they have to know what kind of combination they should use.

There are different types of golf clubs, to make a concrete list we should split them into four groups:

- Woods: Originally made of woods (They are not), these are the clubs that are used to hit the ball the farthest, they are the longest golf clubs (Shaft wise) and have the closest club face (Loft).

- Iron set: the irons are made for intermediate distances, they combined a good length but also, they combined being more accurate than the woods.

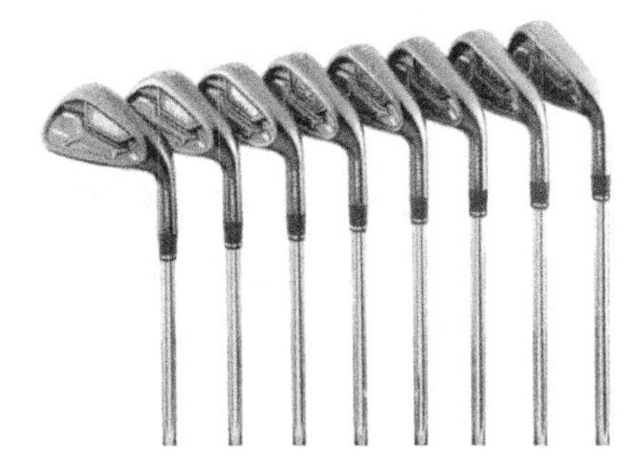

- Wedges: They can also be a part of the iron set, but mostly they are used for accuracy more than distance.

- Putters: This is a very specific club with no loft, it is used over the green, for extremely short distances. The golfer gently hits the ball with them to make it roll into the hole.

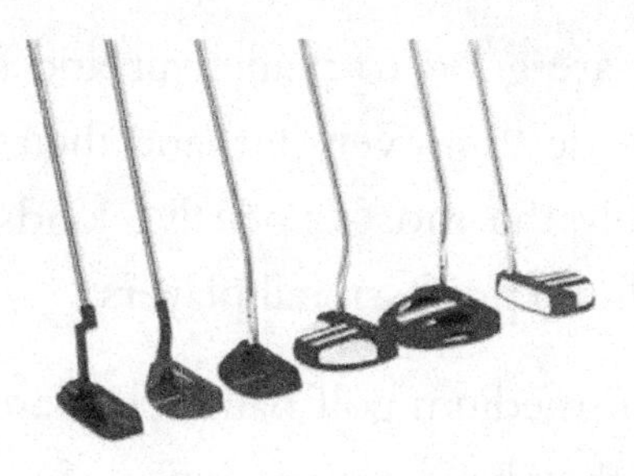

Over time a fifth group began to exist, they are called the hybrids. They are a mix of woods and long irons, giving the golfers a bit of extra distance and they are still very accurate and easy playing golf clubs.

Golf Balls

Like the golf clubs, golfers can only play official golf balls approved by the associations.

Opposite to other sports, in golf the golfer must buy his golf balls, this allows him to choose which kind of golf ball they want to play.

On the outside golf balls are extremely similar, however on the inside, they are quite different, this difference is what makes every golf ball to have different pros and cons.

Over the years golf balls have been improving tremendously, however, like golf clubs, let's try to split them into groups.

- Softballs: These golf balls usually have 3, 4 or more cores, making them very soft on the inside, this allows them to be golf balls that are good to maneuver and stopped. However they are not made to go very far, and their durability is short. They are usually the most expensive kinds of golf balls and also used by all the professional players.

- Intermediate or medium golf balls: They are a mix of softness and hardness, they have a good sense of control, and they go further than the softballs, also they last longer, however, they are not very popular as golfers tend to want a softball if they are looking for control, or a hardball if they are looking for distance, this is something in between.
- Hardballs: The last group of golf balls are the hard ones, they have only 1 or 2 cores, and when hit they go very far, however, they are not very easy to be controlled and especially to stopped. They last very long and are very cheap, however when a golfer becomes better he wants more control than the distance that is why the softballs are the most preferred.

Accessories

There are lots of accessories in golf, most of them are optional and do not change the game itself. However we feel you should know the basics, so, here they are:

- Golf gloves, it is usually worn on the left hand if the golfer is right-handed (Or vice versa) and the main function is to give the golfer a tighter grip and to avoid looseness of the club, especially if it is summer time when golfers tend to sweat.

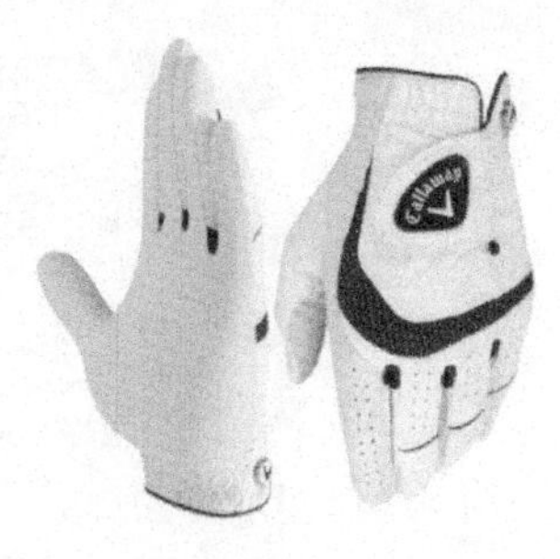

- Golf bags, it is a bag in which the golf clubs, balls, and other accessories are carried. There are mainly two types of golf bags, staffed bags (Or caddie/ cart bags) that do not have any tripod. They are mostly used by golfers who take a caddie (Somebody to help them) or a cart. Or there are stand bags, which they come with an integrated tripod that allows them to stand up by themselves, usually used by golfers who carry their bag.

- Towels, since golf is played over grass there is always mud on the golf course, this mud mess and leaves dirt in the golf ball, so golfers take a towel with them to clean them.

It is very important that you know that even though you can take almost whatever you want with you on the golf course if your ball hits something that is yours, like your bag or towel, you will get penalties strokes, so you have to be very careful with this.

Types of Golf Courses and Golf Holes

Golf Courses

Golf is an extremely popular sport worldwide. There are about 40.000 golf courses around the world. Even though every golf course is different from each other, golf courses can be categorized.

These categorizations aim mostly towards the kind of golf course that you should expect when you are going to play it.

- Links Golf Courses: They are usually very old, but the name means that they were designed on a natural land in which artificial modifications were almost non-existing. The most typical links courses are usually in windy places as trees are ripped away by the high winds, so there is not much room to change the design.

- Parkland Golf Courses: These kinds of courses are more of a newer design, the name remarks that the golf course is going to have lots of trees that were planted on porpoise with the objective of having an artificial design. Golfers must go around the trees to get to the holes.

- Desert Courses: As the name indicates, these golf courses are designed on the desert, so in general the biggest problem is the watering system, they have almost no trees and if they do they are mostly palm trees.

- Mountain Golf Courses: These golf courses are designed in the mountains, and even though they may have lots of trees, their biggest challenge is playing around the extremely hilly ground. That is why they are not considered Parklands.

Golf Holes

Most of the golf courses have 18 holes. However this is not mandatory. There are also nine holes courses, and clubs that have 27, 36, or even more holes, however, this would be considered as having an 18 and a nine hole course, or 18 holes course, etc.

When clubs have less than 18 holes (The most common number would be 9), what the club usually does is that the play some holes two times, on the second time that golfers play the hole, there is usually a small difference either where they star or where they finished it.

Golf holes have different parts.

Every hole begins with a tee box, that is a very well-cut area in which it is mandatory to hit the first shot. There are some symbols that are called tee balls or tee marks that show the players where they should start. Depending on the hole and the golf course there may be more than one tee box for each hole. Each tee will make the hole a different length. Thus it will change the difficulty of that hole. In tournaments, golfers tee off according to their handicap, better golfers tee off from the back while the others tee off from the front.

The final part of the hole, where the actual hole is, it is called "The Green." These areas are cut almost perfect as it is expected for the ball to roll perfectly on them. This is the only part of the golf course in which the player is allowed to pick up the ball for cleaning (After putting a mark to identify where the ball was).

Everything in between is the hole itself. Depending on the design it is going to have a combination of different parts. The first part is called the "Fairway," as the name indicates this is where you want your golf ball to land from your tee shoot. It is fair, as this grass is also cut very short, making hitting the ball easier than other places, however, you are not allowed to move, kick, hump, change, etc. the position of the ball, you must play it as it lies.

On the sides of the fairway, there are different obstacles that try to complicate the golfers round. The first complication to mention is called "The Rough," it is around the fairway, and it consists of grass that is cut higher (Sometimes it is not even cut at all), this brings two main problems, the first one, it is very hard, sometimes impossible to find the golf ball. Secondly, it is much harder to hit the ball from the rough than from the fairway, as when the club enters the deep grass it usually wiggles towards a different direction, making the result of the shot much more unpredictable.

The trees are other obstacles that you will find mostly in the rough area. However some courses do have trees on fairways and golfers have to go around them. The basic problem with the trees is that they are very high and they interfere a lot with the trajectory of the ball.

Lastly, there are what are called hazards. The hazards can be of two types, a water hazard and a sand hazard. As the name indicates the water hazards are filled with water, and if the ball falls in one and cannot be retrieved, the golfer has to play a new one with a stroke penalty.

Sand hazards are called bunkers, and they are filled with sand. Opposite to the water hazards, the ball can be found and played from there. However, it is very difficult to hit from the sand as the impact of the club face towards the sand is very unstable and hard to measure.

There is also one artificial problem in golf courses, it is called Out of Bounds (O.B.), this is basically where the golf course ends. If a golf ball goes out of bounds, for example over the club wall or fence, then the golfer has to put a new ball, he gets a stroke penalty and still has to redo the shot, this is called a stroke plus distance penalty.

Length and Pars

Every golf course has a specific length that is announced either in the hole board or the scorecard that is given at the beginning of the round. Depending on the length how many strokes the hole pretends each golfer should take. This number is called "Par."

There are three kinds of pars, Par 3, Par 4 and Par 5 (Some very weird cases there are Par 6, but it almost never happens). So, if the hole is a par 3, the golfer is expected to finish it in 3 strokes, anything over that is bad and under that is good. Same with the par 4 or 5s. As a rule, golfers usually take two strokes in the green before sinking the ball in the hole this means that if the hole is a par 3, they are expected to reach the green in only one shot, if it is a par 4, only in 2, etc.

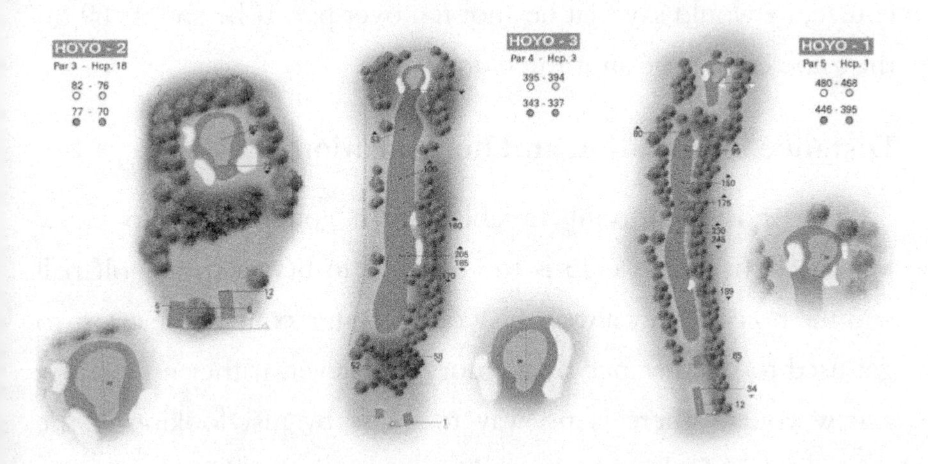

Golf has an official name for each scoring on a hole, and it goes as follows:

One shot - Hole in One

Three shots under par (only possible in par 5s) - Albatross or Double Eagle

Two shots under par - Eagle

One shot under par - Birdie

Even shots - It is called a par

One shot over par - Bogey

Two shots over par - Double bogey

Three shots over par - Triple Bogey and so on.

Most of the golf courses have ten par 4s, four par 3s, and four par 5s. So, if you add this numbers you get the course par, in this case, it is 72 (That is why we subtract 72 strokes from the gross score to get the handicap). If a golfer shoots 82 shots in a par 72 course, he would say that he shot ten over par. If he shoots 69 on the same course, he shot three under par.

Distance information and hole position.

The most important variable that a golfer needs to know before choosing his club is the distance in between his golf ball and the hole. If they always play on the same course, they start to get used to the distance by memory. However, if they are playing a new course, there is no way to guess by just looking at the course. Therefore, clubs have distance marks to show the golfer that information.

Next, to the tee box, there are signs that tell the golfers the hole length. Then on the sides of the fairway, there are usually three sticks that depending on the color (Indicated on the scorecard or board) they indicate 100, 150 and 200 yards to the hole. Plus, some golf courses also have the distance printed on the sprinkles on the grass. Finally, now there are devices with GPS information and capabilities that tells the golfer the exact distance to the hole.

18
Three Ponds
Hole
PAR 4
415
390
370

173 – 195
184

When the golfer looks towards the green, he sees a pin with a flag that shows where the hole is, however from a distance of about 100 yards or more it is very hard to know if the hole is placed in the front, middle or back of the green. This is very important information as the difference of a front pin versus a back pin can be considering making the club selection different. Plus, it may happen that if the pin is short (Front), the obstacles like bunkers can be disturbing more than if the pin is in the back. To let the golfer know the actual placement of the hole, clubs have different ways of telling. The two most common ways are either color flags that show the pin position (Usually is red-front, white-middle, blue-back) or there is a second small flag underneath the big one that depending on how high it is on the pin, how far is the hole on the green.

Playing the Game

The game always begins at the tee off a box on the first hole. From there the job is easy, you just have to sink the ball in the hole following golf rules in as little strokes as possible.

Golf courses rarely start with a par 3, so prepare yourself for a full driver shot on the first hole, warm up on the driving range and be ready, the first shot is probably one of the most important shots in the round as it gives or takes a lot of confidence depending on the result.

If the stroke was successful and you are where you wanted to be, great, follow the same idea for your next shots. However, if you are in the rough, cross bunker, you do not have a clear shot to the green, here is where you will have to haggle with the golf hole. As a general rule remember, the more difficult the shot is, the bigger the award, but the bigger the risk. Always try to think twice if you want to go over the trees towards the green, or just laying it up around the trees towards a safe part of the fairways is good enough. You can always have a nice approach shot or even a good putter to save the par.

Assuming things worked out not bad but not perfect, meaning you are close to the green but not on the green, try to understand the risks of your approach shot. If there are no risks (Especially it is not hilly), then try to go for an aggressive approach to save the par, but if there are some risks, like a hill that can roll your ball towards the water or a bunker in between, maybe it is time for a safer approach and either trying to sink the putter or be happy with a bogey. Always remember, bogey is golf double bogey is hell. Similar with the putter, if you are over a 20ft putter, then trying to sink that putt may be a bad idea, as you may go over a couple of feet and if you "don't come back" you will do the most hated thing in golf, THE THREE PUTTS. Maybe aiming for two putts from the beginning is good enough and smarter.

If things were great on the entire hole and you are already on the green at a close distance to the hole for a nice birdie attempt, then that moment is a good opportunity to go for it. Birdies are a great satisfaction and also big confidence boosters, so they may even help you out more on the next holes than you realize.

Once you have finish hole number one with either way that I have to describe, the job is very easy, just repeat it on the next 17 holes.

At the end of the round, especially if you are playing with your regular friends and are staying for some drinks, comes the part of the "what would have happened" golf. You will only be hearing "if I had sunk the putt on the 13th hole, then the round this and that", truth is golfers are very good at changing the past when it is convenient for them, but they always forget about that lucky bounce on the tree on that hole or the putter that they sunk from more than 30 feet away.

My recommendation for you is, instead of on focusing on something that cannot be changed, try to focus on what you did wrong and what can be improved.

Here are the basic stats you should look out for:

- Numbers of fairways hit, this means how many of your tee-offs in par 4's and 5's went into the fairway. Have in mind that there are usually 14 attempts as four holes are par 3s.
- Numbers of greens hit, how many greens out of the 18 you were on two strokes before the par.
- Numbers of total putters, this one is very self-explanatory, how many times you put the ball on your round.
- Numbers of three putts, this is very important as maybe you have put 30 times which is great, but you also had three putts lots of time, then this is something to improve.

If you have these statistics regularly, you will find out which are your weak points, and of course the ones you will need to work on more, and which are your strengths, meaning that even though you shouldn't forget about them, maybe your time is better to invest on something else.

Different Kinds of Strokes

In golf, there are different kinds of strokes. Even though the main concept is the same on all of them (Hitting the ball as close to the hole as possible) they can be broken into different shots depending on:

- Distance
- Objective
- Effect
- Altitude

Explaining in words golf shot is not very easy. However, we will do our best.

- Golf shots according to distance:
  - Long strokes, like the name, says it, the objective of this shots is to hit the golf ball as far as possible leaving the fewer distance possible in between the hole and the ball for the next shot. We could say that on long strokes you are not able to hit as far as the hole despite how hard you try to hit the ball. These shots are hit with the woods (Driver, 3 wood, 5 wood) and the long irons (2 iron, 3 iron, 4 iron).
  - Medium shots, they are somewhere in between the long shots and the proximity shots. In this kind of shots, the golfer can hit as far as the hole. However, since he knows

he is far and most likely the hole will be protected by bunkers and water hazards, he only tries to hit the green. These medium shots are made with the middle irons (5 iron up to iron number 8)

– Short shots are shots in which the golfer not only has enough strength to hit as far as the hole, but this represents no hard physical effort for him. Thus he will try to get the ball as close to the hole as possible. Taking risks if the hole is protected by water or bunkers must be evaluated on site.

– Approach. The approach is a shot in which the golfer is very close to the pin. Usually not father than 60 yards away. In this shot, the golfer should try to leave the ball as close as possible from the hole even if it means to take risks. Most of the times, these are recovery shot, meaning a previous shot had to go wrong to leave an approach.

– Putting is the final stroke. The golfer will try to roll the ball towards the hole and sink it if possible. It happens mostly on the green (although it can be hit from anywhere) as the green surface is cut extremely even.

- Golf shots according to the objective:

This may sound counterintuitive as the main objective should be to sink the ball or to leave it as close as possible from the hole, right? This is not true, not all shots main objective is that in cases in which you may be in the trees you may have to "lay it up" which means sacrificing distance to go to a safe spot.

Think of it this way; you are 140 yards away from the pin, you have two trees in front of you, going over the trees is not an option as they are too tall. But there are some gaps in between the branches; you have two options, you can try to shoot through them with an obvious risk which is that if the ball hit one of the branches it may bounce even more into the trees. The second option is to go around the tree on a safe path, this way you will not be able to get to the pin, but you will reduce your shot's risk significantly.

- Golf shots according to the effect:

There are four main effects possible when hitting the golf ball that alters the trajectory of the ball.

- Slice, this is when the ball trajectory has a curve shaped like a "C," meaning from left to right.
- Draw (Or pull), is the opposite, the trajectory is an inverted "C," the ball starts going straight and then turns to the left.

If you are left handed, then they are the opposite.

These shots come very in handy when you may have to dodge a tree or water, this way you can try to go around obstacles instead of just going over them.

- Golf shots according to their altitude:

- High shots with backspin. In this kind of shot, the golfer tries to get as much altitude from the shot as possible, usually by opening the club face. In general, the distance will be lost when trying to hit extra high. Also, the golfer tries to put as much backspin as possible on the ball trying to make the landing very soft and then rolling back.

- Low shots (Or punch shots) with forwarding spin. This kind of shots is ideal when you have trees that have some room on their lower part or if you have a lot of wind in your face. Opposite to the high shot, the golfer should try to close the club face and get a low trajectory shot. Have in mind that with these characteristics the golf ball will have a lot of rolls and it will be hard to control.

Scoring and other types of playing

Most common scoring

Match and medal play:

Counting the strokes is always the same, every time you hit the ball it counts as one stroke.

However, depending on the type of golf game that you are playing the overall score may vary.

If you are playing stroke play (despite the amount of players), then you count all the shots that you took to finish all the holes.

If you are playing a match game, then you only count the stokes you took on that hole versus the strokes your competitor had, whoever had the lowest numbers wins the hole and one point (Ties can happen an add 0). The biggest difference in between these two scoring methods is that on the second one if you lose with a difference of one or ten shots it still count as one point. So, in a way, it is more forgiven than stroke play.

Other types of playing

There are more combinations possible than the one we have just mention that depends mostly on how many players per team there are.

Stableford

It is still a single player game with individual points per hole.

- If the player scores a double bogey or worse he gets no points
- If the player scores a bogey, he gets one point
- If the player scores a par, he gets two points
- If the player scores a birdie, he gets three points.
- If the player scores an eagle, he gets four points
- If the player scores a double eagle (3 under par) he gets five points

Then at the end of the round, each player adds their Stableford points and whoever got the most points wins.

If there are two players per team, then they can play these alternative versions.

Fourball - Stroke play - Better ball

In this game, both players play the hole individually, and whoever has the lowest score on that hole is the one that counts. For example, if Allan and Bob are playing hole number one, Allan scores a bogey and Bob a par, then they got a par on the first hole and so on.

Stroke play - Aggregate

Instead of counting the best score, the players have to sum both of their scores, and they have a final number. In the example, if it was a par 4 then Allan had a 5 and Bob had a 4 then they score a 9 (In theory on a par 8, although this is never said).

Stroke play - Foursome

In this kind of game, the players hit the ball one time each. Meaning in hole number one Allan tees off, and despite where the ball ends then Bob hits the second shot and so on. One player will tee off on the odd holes (holes 1, 3, 5, etc.) and the other one on the even holes (holes 2, 4, 6, etc.). An important note, the tee off is never to be altered. Let's say Allan is teeing off on the odd holes and he sinks the last putt on hole number two (An even hole), then if they would have to alternate it would be Bob's turn, however, since the tee off cannot be altered, it is again Allan's turn.

Match Play - Fourball better ball - Aggregate - Foursome

It is the same as before but with the match play rules, meaning instead of playing versus everybody on the golf course and adding their score from each hole. In this scenario, a team A (Allan and Bob) play individual holes versus team B (Chris and Dan), whoever wins the hole gets the point.

Scramble Golf

This type of game is not often played unless is a corporate tournament or a special event. It is designed so that it is very fun and the score is not that important.

It works as follow:

All four players tee off from the first hole (There will be four balls on the hole), then they choose the ball that they consider the best (It doesn't mean it must be the closest to the pin), and then they all play again from there and so on. It is a very fun modality as almost always one of the four players is going to end up in a decent location.

If there is a Scramble team of three or even two players, they are given extra handicap shots to compensate.

Skins

The gambler's choice by far. In this game, a value of either points or money is assigned to each hole. It usually increases towards the end. For a player to win the skin, he has to beat all of the other competitors, meaning if two players tie, then they all tie and the skin is added to the next hole, and so on.

Example:

Skins are worth:

Holes 1 through 6 - 1 point

Holes 7 through 12 - 2 points

Holes 13 through 18 - 3 points

In hole number one, Allan and Bob make a par, then Chris makes a bogey and Dan a double bogey. In this scenario, the skin is tied, and it is added to the next hole, meaning they will be playing for 2 points on hole number two.

If they are playing hole number six, and Chris and Dan get a birdie while Allan and Bob make a double bogey, then the skins go to the next hole which will be worth three points (1 point for the skin on the sixth hole and 2 points for the skin on the seventh hole).

This type of playing is very popular among gamblers as if there are some skins accumulated due to ties there can be a lot of points (or money) at stake, and even worse a player who had extremely bad holes for a while can win all the skins if he has a great hole when he needs to.

Choice score

A player plays more than one round (to be settled by the committee), and then he chooses the best score for each hole.

For example, on hole number one Allan scores a 4 on the first day, and a 3 on the second day, he scores a 3. And it continued throughout the whole golf course.

Mixing types of games

Either for fun or because two tournaments are played at the same time, types of golf rounds or tournaments can be a mix as long as the basic stroke rules apply.

For example, a tournament can be a fourball best ball and aggregate as both players have to hit their ball individually thus complying with the rules in both cases.

However, this is not allowed if they have to play differently, for example, it is not allowed to play fourball best ball and foursome at the same time, as in the first one each player hits his ball and on the second one they have to alternate.

It is very common in a tournament that is played under stroke play, that the players agree to play a parallel fourball for fun, this is allowed and not against the rules.

How much should you practice at the beginning?

This is probably one of the first questions a prospect golfer does to another friend who already plays or a coach that he may know.

Starting a sport is not easy, and golf especially. There are some factors that you have to consider before answering this question.

The first one is of course age. In general, the older you are, the more difficult it is to start things, especially if they involve body/mind coordination. Almost anybody in the world at least once started some activity even if it is minimum next to a child and the child was already a pro in minutes while the grownup is still figuring out how to tie his shoes, right?

Let's assume for this guide, that you are somebody in between the 30-60 years old gap. People in that range will have a similar learning curve.

Second is resources. And it is not only about the money, in resources you have to consider how close you are to golf facilities, the weather in your area and most importantly how much free time you have to start golfing. From all these things, the most important are by far having a decent facility to start.

Why the facility and not time which seems more important? Easy, at the beginning you need to do HIT (High-Intensity Training), meaning practicing for small periods of time but with a lot of intensity. Spending four to six hours on the golf course is not for the beginner.

Lastly would come both your physical body and abilities plus if you have practice a sport before, preferably one that has a similar swing to golf (Like tennis, hockey, baseball, etc.). Playing sports like American Football will not be that much help here.

Of course, we cannot go through every prospect golfer profile, so for the sake of this book, let's say that you are somewhere in the middle of all the things we have mentioned before.

Lastly, what does "the beginning" means? It means from where you start playing golf (Point Zero) up to being able to play your first golf round without further complications (Point Hero). After you got there, then you need a second volume of this guide. It should take an average of about 4-6 months.

A small note here, your friends and teachers may tell you that a regular time frame to get on a golf course is less than 2-3 months. This is a statement we disagree. Playing and completing a successful golf round is not only about hitting the ball in a particular number of strokes, is about knowing the rules, knowing how to behave on the golf course, being prepared. If you go play with your friends, and you hold them back, they have to help you find your ball, explaining the rules, etc. then they will never ask you again, meaning you will most likely quit because of this bad experience.

Week 1-4:

These are probably the most important weeks for a simple reason. It is when most "golfers" quit if they don't like their progress.

On week's 1-4 you should worry about two things.

- Hitting balls
- Hitting them correctly

Of course, we do not mean being with a teacher 24/7, but if you just go practice on your own and you try to figure the swing out by yourself, you will start training and repeating mistakes. These mistakes will go into your muscle memory, and then they will be very hard to rectify in the future.

So, if possible try to go two times a week for just an hour, and only one of those times with a teacher or a friend who is at least a middle or low handicap. Then let them teach you what you should be trying to do and just practice that. Forget about where the golf ball goes, it is not important at this time, as it is doing the right thing. Lastly, if you have the alternative of going more than two days per week, still try not to do it. Golf swing's work with different body muscles than most sports, if you overtrain you have a good possibility of getting an injury, which most likely is going to be either on your hip, elbow or knee. At this time, do not worry about golf rules or having your gear, borrowed gear is enough.

Weeks 5-12

On these weeks, you will see that your golf improvement is very unstable, you will have great days at the driving range and days in which you will just want to quit and never come back.

During this time, try to focus on repetition. You already know what to do, now it is your time to try it on every swing if the ball does not go where you want, or your impacts are not as solid, do not change your swing, keep on going with the good one. This point we can't stress enough, at the beginning, it may happen that some swings that you may feel more comfortable with, may give you better results. However, those swings are not sustainable in the future. I know this rule sounds a bit weird, but, if you are too comfortable, then something must be wrong.

On another plane, this is the time for two things that are parallel to practice. It is a good time to buy your first set of golf clubs. As you have seen in this review, there are so many to choose from. The best thing would be to get a professional idea, in most clubs the golf shops are run by the club pro. Thus, they can let you know what kind of clubs will suit you best.

Finally, now it is time to start learning about golf rules and etiquette. Try to learn the official golf rules book and also if you have friends or a golf club that you can go, try to ask what is common courtesy and etiquette rules. These things may not make you a better hitter, but they will make you a better golfer.

Regarding the amount of practice, you should do per week, feel free to start increasing those numbers a little. Your body should be used to the swing motion, plus you should already know what to look for on your swing.

Weeks 13-24

These final weeks of your "trial period" should be your best, and believe me, you earned them.

At this time, you have a consistent swing, you know about golf rules and etiquette, you have your own gear, and you are free to play as much golf as you want. So, on this time, just enjoyed it. Try to pay more attention to your weak strokes instead of the ones you are comfortable, and try to start getting the feel for your short game.

Repetition is a must, if you start playing less, then your golf swing will get a little bit confused. Try to watch professional golf tournaments and see what those players are doing.

When this period is over, it is time to ask your best golf buddy to take you on the golf course. Let him know that you are ready, that you know how to play golf and more importantly how to behave on the golf course without delaying any other golfers.

Once you have played a couple of rounds, then it is time to sign in for an official handicap. After this, you will be able to play official tournaments.

Tips and tricks

The game begins far before the first hole. Eventually you will discover how golf is a game of routine. This routine will not only happen before every time you hit the ball but also before you play and on the days before your matches.

There is no perfect routine, it is more of a "whatever works for you" kind of thing, but eventually, you will find that some things will help your game and some others won't.

For example, some players need to go to the driving range before playing a golf round, other play bad if they do, the same thing with going into the putting green.

Once you have figure out what is the best routine for you try to follow it as much as possible but always keep an open mind about changing it. Just because is working now, does not mean is going to work in the future.

Other routines that you will need to find on your own are your stroke routine, which means what are you going to do before hitting the ball. Some golfers take two or three practices swings, some golfers more and others left. Again, there is no perfect rule, if you feel comfortable just standing next to the ball and hitting it, do not worry if your golfer's friends are doing three practice swings if the result of your stroke is good, then you are on the right path.

Lastly, it is very important that you figure out how many times during the week you should practice and if this practice will happen at the driving range, on the same golf course you are playing on the weekend, on a different golf course and with or without a coach. I will make a bit of a stronger point here that you should practice at least once (Ideally twice) throughout the week. Of course, this will depend mostly on your time availability and if you have a golf facility next to your home.

Try to go the driving range more than going on the golf course, as the driving range is much more efficient time-wise. Think about it this way:

- On the driving range, in about an hour you can hit 100 balls, this means minimum time consume and high repetition
- On a practice golf round, you will hit 100 balls in 5 hours, as you will be walking 95 % of the time, and only hitting the ball the other 5 %. This makes the system ineffective, it consumes a lot of time, and there is no repetition, as when you hit the ball, it will be at least a couple of minutes before you hit it again.

The only time it makes sense to play a practice round on the golf course is if you haven't played that course lots of time, in this case, it makes sense as you should know how you are going to play the course and for example if on some holes you are going to tee off with an iron or 3-wood instead of a driver. Similar to get the feel of the greens, if they are fast or not. In this case, it makes sense to have some practice on the golf course.

Conclusion

Our conclusion would be just one. Enjoy the game. There is a reason why these sports have become so popular, and it has lasted more than 500 years. Golf will not always treat you right, but it will keep you very happy and entertained.

It is a sport that you will be able to play decently until the end of your life, and it allows for social interaction and chatting with your friends while playing, something that almost no other sport has.

If you don't have your friends nearby, golf is ruled by a culture of friendly and welcoming people, just go to your club or any course that it is nearby, get to the first tee off and just tell the starter you are alone and ready to play. In less than ten minutes you will be walking the fairway with your possible new best friends.

Another great thing about this sport is that no matter how good or bad you are, how old or young, neither your friends level, you will always be able to play versus whoever you want. You will be able to play with your kids, their kids, etc. Golf's handicap allows you to play evenly with the best golfers in your club, plus if you find the golf courses a bit long, you can always tee off from a shorter tee box avoiding you to try so hard.

We did a lot of emphases that you should not just be a good hitter but a good golfer. To achieve this, you need always to be honest and evenly important to know all the rules and always follow club's etiquette rules.

Golf is a journey, not a destination. Travel through it with passion and humility. You will have moments in which you will not be happy with golf, but trust us, we all have been there, and we never regret it. You will never regret it either.

If you enjoyed this book as much as I've enjoyed writing it, you can subscribe* to my email list for exclusive content and sneak peaks of my future books.

Click the link below:
http://eepurl.com/dvdExn

OR

Use the QR Code:

(*Must be 13 years or older to subscribe)

Made in the USA
Las Vegas, NV
17 December 2023

83023790R00038